Inside the NFL

THE
WASHINGTON REDSKINS

BOB ITALIA
ABDO & Daughters

Published by Abdo & Daughters, 4940 Viking Drive, Suite 622, Edina, Minnesota 55435.

Printed in the United States.

Cover Photo credits: Wide World Photos/Allsport
Interior Photo credits: Wide World Photos

Edited by Paul Joseph

Library of Congress Cataloging-in-Publication Data

Italia, Bob, 1955—
      The Washington Redskins / Bob Italia.
            p.   cm. -- (Inside the NFL)
      Includes index.
      Summary: A brief history of the Washington Redskins, focusing on the play of some of their quarterbacks, including Sammy Baugh, Sonny Jurgenson, and Joe Theismann.
      ISBN 1-56239-465-7
      1. Washington Redskins (Football team) -- Juvenile literature. [1. Washington Redskins (Football team) -- History.] I. Title. II. Series: Italia, Bob, 1955— Inside the NFL.
GV956.W3I83   1996
796.332'64'09753--dc20
                                              95-43589
                                                  CIP
                                                      AC

CONTENTS

Late Bloomers

Having joined the National Football League (NFL) in 1932, the Washington Redskins have had a long history. But it wasn't until head coach Joe Gibbs appeared in 1981 that the Redskins experienced their glory days, going to four Super Bowls in ten years and winning three of them.

Washington Redskins' coach Joe Gibbs (center).

Washington has had an impressive cast of players throughout the years. There was quarterback Sammy Baugh, quarterback Sonny Jurgenson, wide receivers Bobby Mitchell and Charley Taylor, running back Larry Brown, linebacker Jack Pardee, defensive lineman Diron Talbert, and safety Richie Petitbon. But despite all these big names, the Redskins rarely made the NFL championship game.

Gibbs changed all that in 1982 when the Redskins won the Super Bowl for the first time—ending a 40-year championship drought. Players like quarterback Joe Theismann, running back John Riggins, and defensive linemen Dexter Manley and Charles Mann made it all possible. In the late 1980s and early 1990s, Washington won two more Super Bowls with a new cast of stars featuring quarterbacks Doug Williams and Mark Rypien.

Gibbs and his star players are gone now as Washington tries to rebuild a championship team. But it may be a long time before the Redskins see another Super Bowl trophy hoisted in their locker room.

**Opposite page:
Quarterback Joe Theismann.**

The Boston Redskins

The Boston Redskins entered the National Football League in 1932. But even though the team played respectably, fans didn't support the team.

The Boston Redskins had powerful running backs like Cliff Battles, Ernie Pinckert, Pug Rentner, and Riley Smith. But they never had an effective quarterback who could get the ball to ends Charlie Malone and Wayne Millner.

In 1936, the Redskins made it all the way to the NFL championship game. But they lost to the Green Bay Packers 21-6. It was the last game the Redskins played in Boston.

The next season, the team moved to Washington, D.C., and became the Washington Redskins. The team received new burgundy jerseys and gold pants. Redskins fans were treated to halftime shows that included fireworks, circus acts, and exotic animals. On the field, the Redskins put on another show.

Before moving the team to Washington, the Redskins signed quarterback Sammy Baugh for the 1937 season. As players go, Baugh was ahead of his time. He had a powerful, accurate arm, and liked to pass more than call running plays. But some observers wondered if Baugh and his passing game was tough enough for the NFL.

The First Championship

It didn't take Baugh long to silence the critics. In 1937, Washington won the Eastern Division title, beating the heavily-favored New York Giants 49-14 in the final game of the regular season to clinch the title. In only their first year in Washington, the Redskins would play in the league championship game.

Washington traveled to Chicago to play the Bears. Again, the Redskins were underdogs. They fell behind 14-7 when Baugh limped into the locker room with an injury. The championship seemed out of reach.

But Baugh returned and riddled the Bears defense for 335 yards and 3 touchdowns. Receiver Wayne Millner caught two long touchdown passes, and the Redskins captured their first NFL championship, 28-21.

In 1940, Baugh led the Redskins to another Eastern Division title and earned the right to play the Chicago Bears for the championship. But this time, the title game had a different result. Chicago coach George Halas unveiled a new alignment known as the T formation, with three backs in a line behind the quarterback. The Redskins did not know how to defend against this formation, and Chicago jumped out to a 7-0 lead.

Baugh drove the Redskins down the field. But receiver Charlie Malone dropped a pass at the goal line. It was the last time they would threaten to score.

The T formation gave the Redskins fits. They could not stop the Bears from scoring. The game ended 73-0 in favor of Chicago—the most lopsided championship game ever.

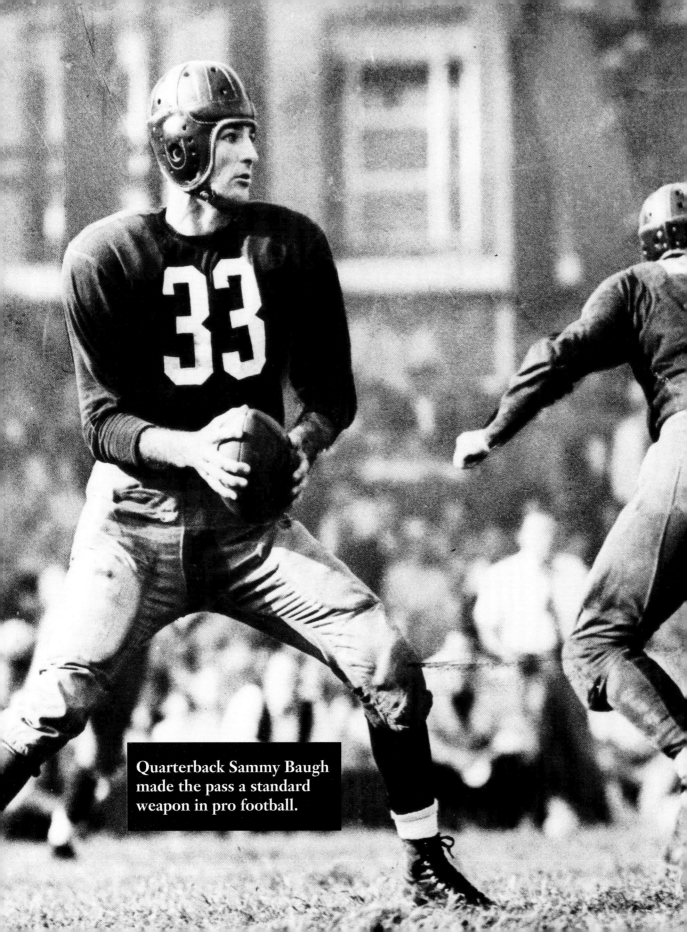

Quarterback Sammy Baugh made the pass a standard weapon in pro football.

Washington rebounded after the devastating defeat. They won the Eastern Division in 1942, 1943, and 1945, and defeated Chicago in the 1942 title game 14-6. But in the 1943 title game, they lost 41-21 to the Bears, and 15-14 to Cleveland in the 1945 championship. During the 1945 season, rookie receiver Steve Bagardus established himself as one of Washington's new talents.

In 1947, Baugh ended his career by throwing six touchdown passes in a 45-21 win over the Chicago Cardinals. During his career, he led the team to five division titles and two NFL championships. But Baugh's departure marked the beginning of a long, dark period for the Redskins. Washington fans would have to wait almost 25 years before their team returned to the playoffs. Except for a 7-7 record in 1966, Washington had a losing season every year from 1956 through 1968.

Sammy Baugh (second from right) plays his last game as a Redskin.

Sonny Jurgenson

In 1964, Washington began to emerge from the darkness when they traded popular quarterback Norm Snead to the Philadelphia Eagles for a Christian Adolph "Sonny" Jurgenson. Jurgenson had a strong arm and was very accurate.

Jurgenson credited his high school coach for his passing ability. His coach, Leon Brogden, developed a drill in which Jurgenson had to get down on one knee and throw the ball. It helped develop the strength in his arm and taught him how to throw hard.

Despite Jurgenson's leadership and talented wide receivers Bobby Mitchell and Charley Taylor, the Redskins still could not break their losing ways. In 1969, the Redskins decided to find a head coach who could recapture the glory days. They hired Vince Lombardi, who had led the Green Bay Packers to five NFL championships and two Super Bowl titles. Lombardi had retired after the 1967 season, but the Redskins offered to make him part-owner and head coach.

When Lombardi took over the Packers, they were one of the worst team in the NFL. In a little more than five years, he molded one of the greatest teams in NFL history.

With Jurgenson at quarterback, Lombardi acquired two running backs—Charlie Harraway and Larry Brown —to bolster the rushing attack. Just before the season opener, Lombardi reminded his players that he had never coached a losing team. The Redskins finished 7-5-2 and hopes were high for the 1970 season.

But 1969 was Lombardi's last season. Before the start of the 1970 season, Lombardi became ill with cancer. Two months later, he was dead. Redskins owner George Marshall also died that year.

Edward Bennett Williams bought the team and hired George Allen as head coach. Allen had built the Los Angeles Rams into an NFL powerhouse. But there was still a lot of work to do.

George Allen

Allen came to the Redskins determined to mold a championship team with experienced players. He traded many draft choices for players who were considered over the hill. That's why people started calling the Redskins the "Over the Hill Gang."

Allen also traded for many players from his old Rams team. Linebacker Jack Pardee, defensive lineman Diron Talbert, and safety Richie Petitbon joined linebacker Chris Hanburger and cornerback Pat Fischer—all over 30 years old—to form a rock solid defense.

The new old Redskins made the playoffs in 1971 with a 9-4-1 record—the team's best mark since 1945. In 1972, quarterback Billy Kilmer and running back Larry Brown led the Redskins to the Eastern Division title. In the first round of the playoffs, the Redskins defeated the Green Bay Packers 16-3. Now they would play the Dallas Cowboys in the NFC championship game.

Dallas had won the last two NFC titles. But against the fired up Over-the-Hill Gang, the Cowboys were trounced 26-3. Incredibly, the Redskins had made it to the Super Bowl. But they had the misfortune to play the undefeated Miami Dolphins. Miami stopped Washington's offense, and the Redskins lost 14-7.

Joe Theismann

Despite their advancing age, the Redskins made the playoffs three of the next four years. But each time, they failed to reach the Super Bowl. After a 9-5 season in 1977, Williams had enough of Allen's reliance on older players. It was time to rebuild with youth. Allen was fired, and Jack Pardee replaced him.

Because Allen used only veterans, young quarterback Joe Theismann sat on the bench while Billy Kilmer and Sonny Jurgenson played. Pardee decided to play Theismann.

Theismann was a mobile quarterback who could beat teams with the run as well as the pass. But he was also undisciplined and made too many mistakes. To improve Theismann's performance, Pardee

Quarterback Joe Theismann.

hired Joe Walton as the Redskins' offensive coordinator in 1978. Walton worked hard with the young quarterback and showed him how he could improve—and improve he did.

As Theismann got better, so did the Redskins. In 1979, they posted a 10-6 record. Running back John Riggins led the ground attack, and rookie wide receiver Art Monk became Theismann's favorite target. Three-hundred-pound Dave Butz anchored the defensive line. Pardee was named NFL Coach of the Year.

But the Redskins improvement came to a sudden halt in 1980 as Washington fell to 6-10. For Pardee, who had played for Washington under George Allen, it was too much to take. He decided to resign.

Joe Gibbs and the Super Bowl

Williams named Bobby Beathard as general manager and Joe Gibbs as head coach. Gibbs had much success in San Diego designing their outstanding passing attack.

Gibbs immediately got the Redskins rolling. In 1982, Washington made the Super Bowl for the second time in their history. The defense, led by defensive linemen Dexter Manley, Charles Mann, and Darryl Grant, gave up the fewest points in the NFL. In the playoffs, Theismann and Riggins led an offense that scored 83 points in 3 playoff-game victories as they won the NFC championship.

Redskins coach Joe Gibbs kneels on the sidelines during the final moments of the NFC Championship game.

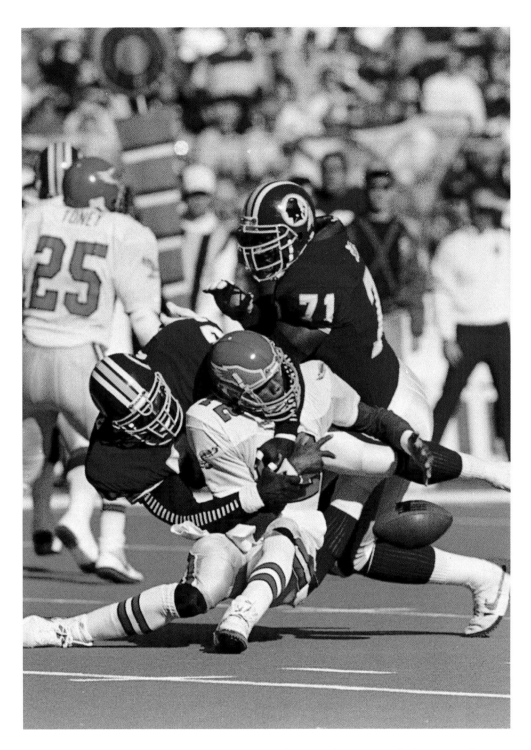

Redskins defenseman Dexter Manley sacks Randall Cunningham.

Running back John Riggins (44) fends off a Dolphin defender.

The Redskins faced the Miami Dolphins in the Super Bowl. It was a rematch of Super Bowl VII ten years earlier. This time, they were ready.

Miami opened the scoring on a long pass. Then they returned a kick off to take a 17-13 lead in the third quarter.

Washington found themselves deep in their own territory. Theismann tried to throw a screen pass over Miami defender Kim Bokamper, but he reached up and deflected the ball high in the air.

Bokamper thought he had an easy interception. But Theismann knocked the ball out of Bokamper's hands—saving a touchdown. Theismann had made the biggest defensive play of the game.

In the fourth quarter, Washington took control. Riggins scored on a long run, and Theismann threw a touchdown pass to Charlie Brown. The final score was 27-17 in favor of Washington. For the first time in 40 years, the Redskins were NFL champs.

In 1983, Theismann had an even better year. Washington finished with a 14-2 record and notched playoff victories over the Los Angeles Rams and San Francisco 49ers. The Redskins had returned to the Super Bowl for the second year in a row. But this time, the Los Angeles Raiders easily handled Washington 38-9.

John Riggins tramples over a Miami Dolphins defender.

10   20   0   5

Joe Theismann leads the Redskins to the Super Bowl in 1982.

WASHIN

REDS

WASHINGTON REDSKINS

Sammy Baugh plays his last game as a Redskin in 1947.

10   40   5

John Riggins joins Washington in 1976.

40   20   10

Williams is named Super
Bowl MVP in 1987.

Art Monk becomes the
NFL's all-time leading
receiver in 1992.

NGTON
KINS

WASHINGTON
REDSKINS

40   30   10

Mark Rypien leads the
Redskins to a Super Bowl
victory in 1991.

Doug Williams

Theismann played two more years with Washington before suffering a broken leg against the New York Giants. Jay Schroeder replaced Theismann, but in 1987, Schroeder was also hurt.

The Redskins had second-year quarterback Mark Rypien on the bench. But Gibbs felt he wasn't ready. Instead, they turned the reins over to Doug Williams.

Williams had been with Tampa Bay in the late 1970s and early 1980s. Then he left the team for the United States Football League (USFL). Three years later, the USFL folded and Williams was looking for work. There were no starting quarterback jobs available in the NFL. The Redskins were the only team that called him.

Williams led the Redskins to the playoffs. Victories over Chicago and Minnesota put Washington into its fourth Super Bowl. This time, they faced the Denver Broncos, who were favored to win the big game. Experts weren't convinced Williams could lead his team to victory when the NFL championship was at stake.

At first, the experts seemed right as the Broncos grabbed a 10-0 lead. But then, Washington exploded for five touchdowns—all in the second quarter. It was the most touchdowns scored in one quarter in Super Bowl history.

The Broncos never recovered from the shock. When the game finally came to an end, Washington recorded an impressive 42-10 triumph.

Williams set several Super Bowl records. He threw for a record-340 yards and tossed a record-tying 4 touchdown passes. His efforts earned him the game's MVP honors. Even more, wide receiver Ricky Sanders and running back Timmy Smith set their own Super Bowl records. Sanders had over 200 receiving yards, and Smith had more than 200 rushing yards.

Doug Williams led the Redskins to the playoffs.

Mark Rypien

In 1988, Williams rise to the top of the NFL ended when he hurt his back midway through the season. Since Schroeder had been traded, it was time for Rypien to step in. He and the offense played well. But injuries decimated the defense as Washington finished 7-9.

In 1989, Rypien won the starting quarterback job. But the team struggled early and was 5-6. Making the playoffs seemed impossible. But in the next game, Rypien completed 30 of 47 passes for 406 yards and 4 touchdowns as Washington defeated Chicago 38-14. It was the turning point of the season.

The Redskins didn't lose again. They finished the season with a 10-6 record and just missed the playoffs. Rypien made the Pro Bowl. In his first full season as a starter, Rypien had become one of the NFL's best quarterbacks. Only legendary quarterback Sammy Baugh had enjoyed such success.

The Redskins were on their way. Besides Rypien, they had one of the best trio of receivers in the league—Art Monk, Gary Clark, and Ricky Sanders. Gerald Riggs and Earnest Byner keyed Washington's powerful rushing attack. Defensive lineman Charles Mann, linebacker Wilbur Marshall, and cornerback Darrell Green made Washington's defense one of the best.

But Joe Gibbs was the real reason Washington had become a championship-caliber team. He had led the team to two Super Bowl titles and three NFC championships. Washington was one of three teams to win at least two Super Bowls during the 1980s. Only Sammy Baugh's Redskins of the 1930s and 1940s had as much success. Washington expected to continue their winning ways into the 1990s.

Redskins quarterback Mark Rypien fades back to pass.

They did just that in 1990, though they never played consistently enough to challenge for the division title. But their 10-6 record was good enough for a return trip to the playoffs.

Washington defeated the Philadelphia Eagles in the first round 20-6. But they were no match for the San Francisco 49ers in round two as they lost 28-10. Suddenly, doubts about Rypien's ability to win the big game surfaced for the following season.

Encore

But in 1991, Rypien was the best quarterback in the league. He threw often to Art Monk, Gary Clark, and Ricky Sanders. Earnest Byner rushed for 1,048 yards, while rookie Ricky Ervins added 680 rushing yards. Gerald Riggs became a goal line specialist, scoring 11 touchdowns. On defense, Wilbur Marshall and Darrell Green made the Pro Bowl. Placekicker Chip Lohmiller led the NFL with 149 points.

In the playoffs, Washington had an easy time with Atlanta as they jumped out to a 14-7 halftime lead and shut the door on the Falcons offense while tacking on 10 second half points. Washington won 24-7.

In the NFC championship game, the Detroit Lions proved to be a much lesser opponent. Though the game was close at halftime, the Redskins broke the game open in the third quarter as they went up 27-10. Washington added another 14 points in the fourth quarter for a 41-10 blowout. The Redskins were going to the Super Bowl for the fourth time in 10 years.

Super Bowl XXVI was close—through the first quarter. Then Rypien picked apart the Buffalo defense for a 17-0 halftime lead. Washington went up 24-0 in the third quarter before Buffalo got on the board with a touchdown and a field goal, making the score 24-10. But then Rypien threw another touchdown pass to put the Redskins up 31-10 heading into the final quarter.

Lohmiller tacked on two more field goals before the Bills tried to rally. But their 14 fourth-quarter points were hardly enough as Washington won handily 37-24.

The defense intercepted four Buffalo passes, tying a Super Bowl record. Joe Gibbs became the third NFL coach to win three Super Bowls. Rypien completed 18 of 33 passes for 292 yards and was named the game's most valuable player. Life was never better for Rypien.

Decline

In 1992, it did not get better. After a long holdout, Rypien finished the season as the lowest-rated quarterback in the NFC. Despite his problems, Art Monk became pro football's all-time leading receiver.

Earnest Byner's season was a reflection on the team. He gained 1,000 yards rushing, then lost a few yards and was injured, finishing the season with 998 yards. The offense scored 185 fewer points than in 1991, and the team was riddled with injuries. Washington won their first-round playoff game against Minnesota, but lost in the second round to the 49ers. Seeing no bright future, Joe Gibbs announced his retirement two months after the season ended. Defensive coordinator Richie Petitbon took charge for the 1993 season.

Washington opened the new season with a surprising 35-16 victory over the Dallas Cowboys. But then they went into a tail spin as they suffered through their worst season in three decades. At one point, they lost six games in a row. Rypien finished the season with only four touchdown passes. Rookie Reggie Brooks was the only bright spot as

Art Monk is hoisted by his teammates after breaking the league record for career receptions.

he rushed for 1,063 yards. Petitbon was fired after the 4-12 season and replaced by Dallas assistant Norv Turner.

Rypien was gone when the 1994 season began, but the Redskins did not rebound. They opened the season with an embarrassing 28-7 loss to Seattle. Quarterbacks John Friesz and Heath Shuler battled for the starting job all season. Friesz threw four touchdown passes in a Week 2 win over the Saints. But the Redskins struggled the rest of the way as they finished 3-13.

§

Having experienced much success in the early 1990s with Joe Gibbs leadership and Mark Rypien's passing, the Redskins suddenly find themselves struggling to rebuild their team. The near future does not look bright. Washington needs help in nearly all areas of play, especially at quarterback and defense. The Redskins have won championships before with great defenses and skillful quarterbacks. Until these key players are added to the team, it may be a while before Washington finds themselves in another Super Bowl.

Heath Shuler.

Richie Petitbon, coaching the Redskins, in 1993.

GLOSSARY

ALL-PRO—A player who is voted to the Pro Bowl.

BACKFIELD—Players whose position is behind the line of scrimmage.

CORNERBACK—Either of two defensive halfbacks stationed a short distance behind the linebackers and relatively near the sidelines.

DEFENSIVE END—A defensive player who plays on the end of the line and often next to the defensive tackle.

DEFENSIVE TACKLE—A defensive player who plays on the line and between the guard and end.

ELIGIBLE—A player who is qualified to be voted into the Hall of Fame.

END ZONE—The area on either end of a football field where players score touchdowns.

EXTRA POINT—The additional one-point score added after a player makes a touchdown. Teams earn extra points if the placekicker kicks the ball through the uprights of the goalpost, or if an offensive player crosses the goal line with the football before being tackled.

FIELD GOAL—A three-point score awarded when a placekicker kicks the ball through the uprights of the goalpost.

FULLBACK—An offensive player who often lines up farthest behind the front line.

FUMBLE—When a player loses control of the football.

GUARD—An offensive lineman who plays between the tackles and center.

GROUND GAME—The running game.

HALFBACK—An offensive player whose position is behind the line of scrimmage.

HALFTIME—The time period between the second and third quarters of a football game.

INTERCEPTION—When a defensive player catches a pass from an offensive player.

KICK RETURNER—An offensive player who returns kickoffs.

LINEBACKER—A defensive player whose position is behind the line of scrimmage.

LINEMAN—An offensive or defensive player who plays on the line of scrimmage.

PASS—To throw the ball.

PASS RECEIVER—An offensive player who runs pass routes and catches passes.

PLACEKICKER—An offensive player who kicks extra points and field goals. The placekicker also kicks the ball from a tee to the opponent after his team has scored.

PLAYOFFS—The postseason games played amongst the division winners and wild card teams which determines the Super Bowl champion.

PRO BOWL—The postseason All-Star game which showcases the NFL's best players.

PUNT—To kick the ball to the opponent.

QUARTER—One of four 15-minute time periods that makes up a football game.

QUARTERBACK—The backfield player who usually calls the signals for the plays.

REGULAR SEASON—The games played after the preseason and before the playoffs.

ROOKIE—A first-year player.

RUNNING BACK—A backfield player who usually runs with the ball.

RUSH—To run with the football.

SACK—To tackle the quarterback behind the line of scrimmage.

SAFETY—A defensive back who plays behind the linemen and linebackers. Also, two points awarded for tackling an offensive player in his own end zone when he's carrying the ball.

SPECIAL TEAMS—Squads of football players that perform special tasks (for example, kickoff team and punt-return team).

SPONSOR—A person or company that finances a football team.

SUPER BOWL—The NFL Championship game played between the AFC champion and the NFC champion.

T FORMATION—An offensive formation in which the fullback lines up behind the center and quarterback with one halfback stationed on each side of the fullback.

TACKLE—An offensive or defensive lineman who plays between the ends and the guards.

TAILBACK—The offensive back farthest from the line of scrimmage.

TIGHT END—An offensive lineman who is stationed next to the tackles, and who usually blocks or catches passes.

TOUCHDOWN—When one team crosses the goal line of the other team's end zone. A touchdown is worth six points.

TURNOVER—To turn the ball over to an opponent either by a fumble, an interception, or on downs.

UNDERDOG—The team that is picked to lose the game.

WIDE RECEIVER—An offensive player who is stationed relatively close to the sidelines and who usually catches passes.

WILD CARD—A team that makes the playoffs without winning its division.

ZONE PASS DEFENSE—A pass defense method where defensive backs defend a certain area of the playing field rather than individual pass receivers.

INDEX